PROTECTING *YOUR* CHILDREN'S IRA INHERITANCE

with a Retirement Protector Trust

Brenda Geiger, J.D.

Copyright © 2015 by Brenda Geiger

All rights reserved. No part of this book may be used or reproduced in any manner whatsoever without written permission of the author. Published 2015.

Printed in the United States of America.

Paperback:
ISBN: 978-1-63385-037-8

Hardback:
ISBN: 978-1-63385-051-4

Designed and published by

Word Association Publishers
205 Fifth Avenue
Tarentum, Pennsylvania 15084

www.wordassociation.com
1.800.827.7903

Disclaimer

This book is not intended to be legal advice. The information contained within this book is for educational purposes only. Before making any legal decisions, you should first consult a qualified attorney.

contents

Introduction on How Retirement Plans
Intersect with Estate Planning 1

IRA Required Minimum Distribution Rules
for the Original Owner 3

RMD and Stretch-Out Rules for a
Non-Spousal Beneficiary 7

Who or What Should be the Beneficiary
of Your Retirement Account? 11

The Issue of Creditor Protection: Clark v. Rameker
(2014 U.S. Supreme Court Ruling) 15

How to Protect Your Children from Future Lawsuits,
Bankruptcy Creditors, and Divorcing Spouses and
Ensure Stretch Out of Your IRA or 401K 19

What is a "Trust Protector" and How
Can One Help Your Family? 25

Who is a Retirement Protector Trust™ Right for? 29

Real Life Case Examples 31

What is the Process to Set up a Retirement
Protector Trust™? 43

Operating Guidelines for Your Retirement
Protector Trust™ 45

About the Author 51

chapter one

Introduction on How Retirement Plans Intersect with Estate Planning

Today, retirement plans such as IRAs, 401(k)s, 403(b)s, etc. represent the bulk of many people's estates. Therefore, careful planning for what happens to these accounts upon death is required. In the chapters that follow, we will explore the various options for naming a successor on your retirement accounts as well as the benefits and drawbacks. Most people are painfully unaware of the risks of bad planning or no planning for these types of assets. The aim and mission of this book is to provide you with a condensed plain English education on the intersection between retirement plans and estate planning, mainly as it affects children and grandchildren or other non-spouse beneficiaries. Knowledge is power. My hope in writing this book is to give you the knowledge that you need to make informed decisions about your retirement accounts and how they will be passed on to others down the road.

chapter two

IRA Required Minimum Distribution Rules for the Original Owner

Years ago when the IRS first allowed people to set up IRAs and 401(k)s, the idea was that they would be used to augment their incomes in retirement years in addition to social security and they would consume these accounts by the time they passed away. However, now we are seeing that much of America's wealth is tied up in these types of accounts and the balances are so large that most will never consume all of their accounts. In fact, according to a recent Investment Institute Study, more than 1/3 of all household financial assets are held in IRAs and other retirement plans.

Your retirement plans may represent your largest asset and they deserve careful planning with regard to your estate plan. As we'll discuss in a later chapter, there is much concern over whether your children will deliberately or intentionally blow the stretch-out opportunity and accelerate all of the income from your retirement plans and cause themselves more than a 50% reduction in the account value due to income taxes (based on current income tax rates–2015).

As you are likely aware, your IRA or 401(K) had a beneficiary form that you filled out when you set up the account. What you may not realize is that you might have the wrong beneficiaries in place or not set up in the best way to secure the maximum growth potential and asset protection for your beneficiaries. In later chapters, we will explore these options for maximizing the stretch out and asset protection of your retirement accounts for your beneficiaries.

But first, let's discuss how the Required Minimum Distribution (RMD) rules work. RMD rules apply to all qualified plans, 401(K)s, IRAs (including Roth IRAs), deferred compensation plans under IRC section 457, and IRC section 403B annuity contracts. This also applies to corporate plans too – (IRC 402(c)(11), IRS Notice 2007-7).

The original owner of the retirement account is required to take a Required Minimum Distribution (RMD) by April 1st in the year following the calendar year in which the IRA owner reaches the age of 70 ½. In order to determine what the RMD is, you use what's called the Uniform Life Table in the IRS code. It's for use by married owners, married owners whose spouses are not more than 10 years younger, and married IRA owners who spouses are not the sole beneficiary of their IRAs. For example, at the age of 70½, under the Uniform Life Table, the current life expectancy is 27.4. This means that at that age, the original owner of the IRA must divide the balance of his or her account by 27.4 to come up with the Required Minimum Distribution for that particular year. By example, at the age of 71, the divisor is 26.5. For convenience, I have included the Uniform Life Table below:

Uniform Life Table			
Age of IRA Owner/Plan Participant	Life Expectancy (in years)	Age of IRA Owner/Plan Participant	Life Expectancy (in years)
70	27.4	93	9.6
71	26.5	94	9.1
72	25.6	95	8.6
73	24.7	96	8.1
74	23.8	97	7.6
75	22.9	98	7.1
76	22.0	99	6.7
77	21.2	100	6.3
78	20.3	101	5.9
79	19.5	102	5.5
80	18.7	103	5.2
81	17.9	104	4.9
82	17.1	105	4.5
83	16.3	106	4.2
84	15.5	107	3.9
85	14.8	108	3.7

86	14.1	109	3.4
87	13.4	110	3.1
88	12.7	111	2.9
89	12.0	112	2.6
90	11.4	113	2.4
91	10.8	114	2.1
92	10.2	115	1.9

Also, in any given tax year while the IRA account is required to be in payout status (meaning where RMDs are required), if less than the Required Minimum Distribution is taken out of the account, a 50% penalty tax must be paid on the shortfall. The tax must be reported on an IRS form 5329 called Additional Taxes Attributable to IRAs. However, it may be possible to get a waiver from these penalties if you can show to the satisfaction of the IRS that the distribution that wasn't made during the tax year was due to a reasonable error and reasonable steps are being taken to remedy the error. If you encounter this problem, you should consult your CPA or tax advisor. Note, if you have inherited an IRA, you need to make sure the full RMD that the original owner was required to take out in the year of death was withdrawn from the account to avoid penalties (if the account was required to be in payout status).

chapter three

RMD and Stretch-Out Rules for Your Children or Other Beneficiaries

Many people are unaware that their retirement accounts can be stretched out after their death by their children based on their <u>child's</u> life expectancy, IRC 401 (a)(9) (2003) if their child is the designated beneficiary of the account. However, in order for this to happen, your child must start taking RMDs by December 31st in the year following your death.

If the retirement plan owner dies before his or her required beginning date, for example before 70 ½, then there are three possibilities for the account pay out to a non-spousal beneficiary. The first option is to take the entire account, accelerate it and pay the income tax. The second option is a five-year pay out under IRC section 402(A)(9)(B)(ii). The third option is to use the life expectancy of the designated beneficiary as the measuring life for a stretch-out of the retirement account. However, beware of optional plan provisions that provide for a five-year or shorter rule for distributions. If there are optional plan provisions, those rules apply.

So who is a "designated beneficiary"? Under treasury regulation section 1.401 (a)(9)(4), a designated beneficiary must be named as a designated beneficiary under the terms of the plan or by affirmative election by the employee. A designated beneficiary need not be specified by name, but must be identifiable on the date of death of the original plan participant. The designated beneficiary may also be a class of beneficiaries capable of expansion or contraction, such as "my children". The designated beneficiary must be an individual alive on the date of death of the original retirement plan owner. *The designated beneficiary may also be an individual named as a beneficiary of a qualifying trust.*

So who is not considered a designated beneficiary? Examples of those who are not designated beneficiaries include your estate, a charity, a non-qualifying trust, any non-individual other than a qualifying trust, or an individual born after the date of the plan participant's death.

Next, let's examine what date a designated beneficiary must be determined by. A designated beneficiary must be identified by September 30th of the calendar year following the original plan participant's death. As mentioned above, when a non-spousal beneficiary inherits an IRA, 401(k), or other retirement account, they must commence RMDs on or before December 31st of the year following the original plan participant's death in order to utilize the stretch-out option.

For a spousal beneficiary, unless it's a rollover, the spouse must withdraw RMDs on or before the later of December 31st of the year after the original plan participant's death or by December 31st of the year that the original plan participant would have attained the age of 70 ½.

So what happens if you have multiple beneficiaries of your IRA or 401(K) that are not a spouse? If there is just one account, then you need to look to the oldest designated beneficiary to determine the life expectancy and what the RMD will be. Then, that RMD will be divided by the number of beneficiaries on the account. However, if there are separate accounts divided from the same IRA or 401(k), each designated beneficiary can receive his or her portion over his or her life expectancy. This achieves the maximum stretch-out so it's wise to use separate accounts. So a planning tip is if a beneficiary designation names multiple beneficiaries at the plan participant's death, separate accounts should be created. Consultation with your estate attorney and CPA is highly recommended to accomplish this or if you are the beneficiary of one of these types of accounts. I have also included the IRS Single Life

Table below which outlines the Required Minimum Distribution schedule for an inherited IRA by a non-spousal beneficiary.

Single Life Expectancy Table

Final MRD Regulations: Life Expectancy Table

Age	Life Expectancy Factor	Age	Life Expectancy Factor	Age	Life Expectancy Factor
0	82.4	38	45.6	76	12.7
1	81.6	39	44.6	77	12.1
2	80.6	40	43.6	78	11.4
3	79.7	41	42.7	79	10.8
4	78.7	42	41.7	80	10.2
5	77.7	43	40.7	81	9.7
6	76.7	44	39.8	82	9.1
7	75.8	45	38.8	83	8.6
8	74.8	46	37.9	84	8.1
9	73.8	47	37.0	85	7.6
10	72.8	48	36.0	86	7.1
11	71.8	49	35.1	87	6.7
12	70.8	50	34.2	88	6.3
13	69.9	51	33.3	89	5.9
14	68.9	52	32.3	90	5.5
15	67.9	53	31.4	91	5.2
16	66.9	54	30.5	92	4.9
17	66.0	55	29.6	93	4.6
18	65.0	56	28.7	94	4.3
19	64.0	57	27.9	95	4.1
20	63.0	58	27.0	96	3.8
21	62.1	59	26.1	97	3.6
22	61.1	60	25.2	98	3.4
23	60.1	61	24.4	99	3.1
24	59.1	62	23.5	100	2.9
25	58.2	63	22.7	101	2.7
26	57.2	64	21.8	102	2.5
27	56.2	65	21.0	103	2.3
28	55.3	66	20.2	104	2.1
29	54.3	67	19.4	105	1.9
30	53.3	68	18.6	106	1.7
31	52.4	69	17.8	107	1.5
32	51.4	70	17.0	108	1.4
33	50.4	71	16.3	109	1.2
34	49.4	72	15.5	110	1.1
35	48.5	73	14.8	111+	1.0
36	47.5	74	14.1		
37	46.5	75	13.4		

chapter four

Who or What Should Be the Beneficiary of Your Retirement Account?

If you are married, you may be required to list your spouse as the primary beneficiary on your retirement account if you are a California state resident due to community property laws. However, if your spouse executes a waiver, you may be able to change who the primary beneficiary is. But assuming you would like to list your spouse as the primary beneficiary of your retirement account, there are some attractive rollover features for deferral of the account for your spouse. The analysis, however, doesn't stop here.

You must also consider who or what is best to list as the "contingent" beneficiary of your account. If your children are minors, you will not want to list them directly on the beneficiary form. The reason for this is that most custodians will not make a distribution from your retirement account directly to a minor. They will require a court appointed Guardian who is authorized to receive the distribution on behalf of your minor child. Then, once your child reaches the age of 18, they may withdraw the total amount from the account if the appointed Guardian executed a stretch out of the account. We will discuss in a later chapter a way that is much safer and can protect your children (minor or adult) from creditors, lawsuits, predators, divorcing spouses, and bankruptcy.

Many beneficiaries, especially young adults, tend to accelerate IRA distributions by taking the lump sum distribution from the account instead of stretching it. This is what we call "the beneficiary destroying the plan". Even if you have a responsible party that becomes a court appointed Guardian ad Litem for your child, you cannot count on the plan custodian to inform your Guardian that they may stretch the account for your child's benefit. This is what we call "the plan custodian destroying the plan".

You may be wondering why the custodian would want to destroy the plan and not tell your child or your child's Guardian that he or she is entitled to a stretch-out based on their life expectancy? Well the answer is quite simple, especially if you have more than one child. The plan custodian has to report to the IRS and to the new owner of the retirement account in many different fashions throughout the year. If the account gets split into separate accounts, they have to do the same amount of work multiple times over. The plan custodian must track all account balances including increases and decreases, calculate the RMDs based on the life expectancy of the new account holders, mail distributions to the account holders, report account balances to the new account holders and also to the IRS, report distributions to new account holders and to the IRS, and mail information reports to the new account holders and to the IRS annually. This destroys the cost structure for the plan custodian. So relying on the plan custodian to inform your child's Guardian or your adult child that they're entitled to a stretch-out is not wise.

If your child is over 18, the fear is also that they may withdraw the entire balance of the account and accelerate the income in one year. If your aggregated IRA and 401(k) accounts are large ($300,000 or more), this could put your child into the largest tax bracket. If they live in California, that's over 56% in income taxes that will chop your account right in half. For many beneficiaries, they did not work to earn the money in those accounts and it is what we call "found money". Most beneficiaries (regardless of age) are in a car dealership within 72 hours of inheriting any money and they want their new car now.

If stretch-out is desired, it is best to be very careful with the planning and updating of your beneficiary designation form. Also, upon death, the beneficiary will not want to re-title the IRA or 401(k) directly into their name if they are listed directly as the beneficiary before consulting a more sophisticated estate planning attorney. If they do, it will accelerate all of the income in the account and the income tax will be due in the year of withdrawal (for non-Roth IRAs). Think of it like toothpaste in a tube. Once it is out, it's out. You can't stuff it back into that preferred tax-deferred environment.

chapter five

The Issue of Creditor Protection for the Beneficiary of an Inherited IRA Clark v. Rameker (2014 U.S. Supreme Court Ruling)

A recent U.S. Supreme Court case, decided June 12, 2014, clearly delineated by <u>unanimous vote</u> that an inherited IRA is <u>not</u> an exempt asset protected from creditors under federal bankruptcy law. Specifically, the petitioner in this case filed for Chapter 7 bankruptcy and sought to exclude about $300,000 of an inherited IRA that came from her late mother from the petitioner's bankruptcy creditors. She claimed the IRA was an exempt asset under the bankruptcy code from her creditors. After about four years of winding its way up to the U.S. Supreme Court, the court held unanimously that an inherited IRA does not share the same characteristics as a "traditional IRA" and therefore it wasn't an exempt asset. The court held "Funds held in inherited IRAs are not "retirement funds" within the meaning of § 522 (b)(3)(C)."- 573 U.S. (2014) *Clark v. Rameker.*

The court reasoned that "the ordinary meaning of "retirement funds" is properly understood to be sums of money set aside for the day an individual stops working. Three legal characteristics of inherited IRAs provide objective evidence that they do not contain such funds. First, the holder of an inherited IRA may never invest additional money in the account. 266 S.C. § 219 (d) (4). Second, holders of inherited IRAs are required to withdraw money from the accounts, no matter how far they are from retirement. §§408 (a)(6), 401(a)(9)(B). Finally, the holder of an inherited IRA may withdraw the entire balance of the account at any time and use it for any purpose- without penalty." 573 U.S. (2014)

What all this means is pretty much what we already knew- that there is no creditor protection for beneficiaries that are directly listed on a retirement account beneficiary form. For years, I've been drafting Retirement Protector Trusts™ in order to help my clients give their children creditor protection and a paycheck for life. This special trust designed specifically for retirement accounts acts as a shield between the retirement account itself and the beneficiary and their creditors. What's even more is that we can protect the RMDs that come out of the account annually if we need to by granting the Trustee the power to "accumulate" the RMDs inside the trust either directly or by allowing a Trust Protector to switch on this power. There are a few different ways to get to this result, but the most common way is to draft the trust as a "conduit" trust and grant a Trust Protector the power to switch to "accumulation" provisions within 9 months of date of death of the original owner. This gives us the most flexibility because by having the RMD pass through the trust via a conduit to the beneficiary, there is a greater tax efficiency- the RMD is taxed at the beneficiary's personal income tax rate-not at trust income tax rates. But, if we have a creditor issue and the RMD is large, we may prefer to pay additional taxes and accumulate to protect the RMD as well as the undistributed principal of the retirement account.

chapter six

How to Protect Your Children from Future Lawsuits, Bankruptcy Creditors, and Divorcing Spouses and Ensure Stretch Out of Your IRA or 401(K)

Basically, a Retirement Protector Trust™ acts as a shield or barrier to insulate the principal of your IRA, 401(k) or other retirement account from the trust beneficiary's creditors, a bankruptcy, a lawsuit, or a divorcing spouse. This is accomplished by having the Retirement Protector Trust™ itself as the primary or contingent beneficiary of your retirement account and by having no demand rights listed in the trust document itself. The reason a stand-alone trust for your retirement accounts is preferred is because of some provisions in your regular revocable trust that can interrupt your successor Trustee's ability to stretch out the account. For example, the payment of funeral expenses, taxes and other final expenses upon your death can be problematic. In a stand-alone Retirement Protector

Trust™, we do not include these provisions so we avoid any potential issue on that front.

Just to be clear, the trust never becomes the owner of your retirement account. It is simply the receptacle (the beneficiary) for the Required Minimum Distribution (RMD) or if partially or fully accelerated, the money distributed from the account. Who you select as your Trustee and the provisions drafted in the trust for the beneficiary will govern what happens when and whether there is creditor protection for your child or other beneficiary. The Retirement Protector Trust™ is a specialty trust which not all practitioners are versed in drafting due to its complexity.

Some clients may wish to give their children the opportunity to control the trust as a beneficiary-controlled trust at some point in the future (for example, at the age of 35 or 40). Others may wish to force the stretch-out of their retirement accounts and not allow their children the opportunity to withdraw more than the Required Minimum Distribution ever. There is no right or wrong way to draft the trust, but there are preferred methods. Your particular situation, your thoughts and feelings on this topic and sound advice from a skilled and competent estate planning attorney will govern how the trust should ultimately be drafted.

One caution however, if you do make the trust beneficiary-controlled at a stated age and your child experiences a bankruptcy or other creditor issue, they should resign as Trustee immediately and replace themselves with a third-party independent Trustee to prevent a creditor from stepping in their shoes and accelerating the account.

Another unique benefit of the Retirement Protector Trust™ is that you may list several beneficiaries. Each may also have distinct trust provisions. This may become important especially if there is a special-needs beneficiary, a minor beneficiary, one with a drug or alcohol problem, or poor spending habits.

Next, let's look at how the trust works in a practical sense. If you are married, we will want to set up a stand-alone Retirement Protector Trust™ for you and one for your spouse. This is because we don't know who will pass first and because of the complexity of the IRA rules and who the accounts will be rolled over to down the road. After you and your spouse are both gone, your retirement accounts will designate your Retirement Protector Trust™ as the beneficiary of the account. The Trustee of your Retirement Protector Trust™ will have an opportunity to stretch-out the account on behalf of your children or other beneficiaries.

If your beneficiary form lists your Retirement Protector Trust™ with separate accounts for each trust beneficiary, the Trustee can separate the account into shares and stretch based on each beneficiary's life expectancy. This provides for the maximum stretch-out versus just stretching based on the oldest beneficiary's life expectancy (if just the trust itself is listed on the beneficiary form). I prepare the beneficiary form for my clients to ensure that this key step is properly done.

Then, the Trustee divides the account balance by the divisor for that particular beneficiary's share of the account based on their age in the year that the original owner died. For convenience, I have included the IRS Single Life Table below to help you figure out the divisor. For example, if you have two children as the beneficiaries of your Retirement Protector Trust™ and they inherit at the ages of 50 and 55, and your IRA has a $1 million balance, the RMD that must be distributed to your Retirement Protector Trust™ by December 31st of the year after your death is **$14,619.88** for your younger child ($500,000 divided by 34.2) and **$16,891.89** for your older child ($500,000 divided by 29.6).

Single Life Expectancy Table

Final MRD Regulations: Life Expectancy Table					
Age	Life Expectancy Factor	Age	Life Expectancy Factor	Age	Life Expectancy Factor
0	82.4	38	45.6	76	12.7
1	81.6	39	44.6	77	12.1
2	80.6	40	43.6	78	11.4
3	79.7	41	42.7	79	10.8
4	78.7	42	41.7	80	10.2
5	77.7	43	40.7	81	9.7
6	76.7	44	39.8	82	9.1
7	75.8	45	38.8	83	8.6
8	74.8	46	37.9	84	8.1
9	73.8	47	37.0	85	7.6
10	72.8	48	36.0	86	7.1
11	71.8	49	35.1	87	6.7
12	70.8	50	34.2	88	6.3
13	69.9	51	33.3	89	5.9
14	68.9	52	32.3	90	5.5
15	67.9	53	31.4	91	5.2
16	66.9	54	30.5	92	4.9
17	66.0	55	29.6	93	4.6
18	65.0	56	28.7	94	4.3
19	64.0	57	27.9	95	4.1
20	63.0	58	27.0	96	3.8
21	62.1	59	26.1	97	3.6
22	61.1	60	25.2	98	3.4
23	60.1	61	24.4	99	3.1
24	59.1	62	23.5	100	2.9
25	58.2	63	22.7	101	2.7
26	57.2	64	21.8	102	2.5
27	56.2	65	21.0	103	2.3
28	55.3	66	20.2	104	2.1
29	54.3	67	19.4	105	1.9
30	53.3	68	18.6	106	1.7
31	52.4	69	17.8	107	1.5
32	51.4	70	17.0	108	1.4
33	50.4	71	16.3	109	1.2
34	49.4	72	15.5	110	1.1
35	48.5	73	14.8	111+	1.0
36	47.5	74	14.1		
37	46.5	75	13.4		

If the trust is drafted as a conduit trust, the Trustee will pay the RMD out directly to your children (or their guardian) through the trust and each child will report the distribution to the IRS on their individual 1040 income tax return for that year. If the Trustee has the power to accumulate inside the trust, her or she may hold onto the Required Minimum Distribution and invest it inside the trust providing additional creditor protection for the RMD as well as the principal balance for your child from their creditors, lawsuits, a bankruptcy, or a divorcing spouse. Below is a sample design of one way the trust can be set up for a married couple.

Retirement Protector Trust™ For a Married Couple

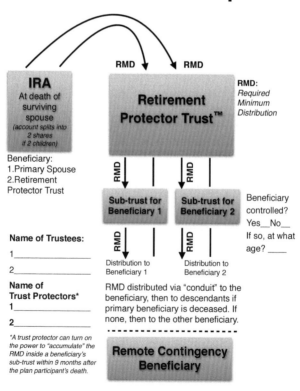

chapter seven

What is a Trust Protector and How Can One Help Your Family?

A Trust Protector is an individual nominated in your trust document that has limited powers to do certain things in relation to the trust if the need arises in the future. The Trust Protector is an old role that was often used in offshore trust planning, which was generally intended to watch over the Trustee, given the ability to react to unforeseen circumstances, and fulfill the original Trust Grantor's intent. More modernly, Trust Protectors are frequently used in domestic trusts, typically in the irrevocable trust context, but may also be drafted into revocable trusts as well.

The role of the Trust Protector has expanded in domestic trust planning over the years. The Trust Protector's authority is generally what is drafted into the trust agreement and he or she can act in a fiduciary or non-fiduciary capacity. Most often they serve in a non-fiduciary capacity without obligation to monitor the Trustee of the Trust. They can be given the authority to do things such as remove and replace a Trustee, fill a Trustee vacancy, update limited provisions in the trust agreement (i.e., tax provisions), move the trust situs (location of administration) to another state for more favorable tax treatment or asset protection, interpret trust terms, settle disputes between co-Trustees, and limit Trustee compensation, among other things.

In the context of a Retirement Protector Trust™, a Trust Protector can also switch on certain powers that will allow the Trustee to "accumulate" the Required Minimum Distribution (RMD) in a sub-trust for a beneficiary. In a 2005 Private Letter Ruling (PLR 200537144), the IRS allowed a Trust Protector to switch the Trustee's "conduit" power to an "accumulation" power inside of a Retirement Plan Trust. By switching to an accumulation power, the Trustee had the ability to forgo distributing the RMDs to the beneficiary, thereby creditor protecting the RMDs from the beneficiary's creditors, a bankruptcy or from the possible reach of a divorcing spouse. This is also extremely important if the beneficiary is the recipient of public benefits such as Medicaid or SSI. A distribution of an RMD could make that type of beneficiary ineligible for a public benefit if the RMD is distributed directly to them. For example, recipients of Medicaid in California cannot own more than $2,000 in assets in order to qualify for Medicaid. The Trustee may still use the RMD "for the benefit of" a special needs beneficiary, but would do so by paying for things indirectly, and not directly to the beneficiary. Another issue that could come up is a beneficiary that is unmotivated to become a productive citizen, a young or immature beneficiary, or one who has drug or alcohol issues.

So at this point you are probably thinking, "Great, it sounds like a good idea to have a Trust Protector on board, but who should I choose to act in that capacity in my Retirement Protector Trust™?" The answer is that it should be someone that is not directly related to you or subordinate to you in your place of business. Typical Trust Protectors include attorneys, CPAs, Enrolled Agents, more sophisticated business associates, and sometimes friends or more remote family members. There are some private fiduciaries, banks and trust companies willing to act in this capacity as well but you will need to check with them first to see if they are willing to serve before you nominate them in your trust document. It is also possible to name a back up to this person or entity or to nominate a Trust Protector designator. A Trust Protector designator is just like it sounds. This individual has the power to later nominate who the Trust Protector will be (usually only if the need arises down the road). Trust Protectors are great in the sense that they can help solve many different types of unforeseen problems that could come up down the road—and flexibility is the key.

chapter eight

Who is a Retirement Protector Trust™ Right for?

The Retirement Protector Trust™ is right for married couples or single individuals with total retirement accounts valued at $200,000 or more who have children, grandchildren, or other beneficiaries for whom they'd like to protect and provide a paycheck for life (or in the case of a minor child, $100,000 or more in combined retirement accounts).

If you like the idea of stretching out your retirement account into 3-9x or more over the life of your child or other beneficiary and protecting them from creditors, bankruptcy, predators, and divorcing spouses, you should invest in this planning. It will also be right for you if you are concerned about protecting your beneficiaries from:

- Blowing the stretch out of your accounts
- Poor money management
- Spending habits

- A child's spouse taking half in a divorce
- A young, elderly, or disabled beneficiary's inability to manage their own financial affairs
- A beneficiary losing their government benefits because of the inheritance
- A second estate tax if passed down to a grandchild (GST tax)
- Lawsuits or creditors of your child
- Bankruptcy of your child
- A child's drug or alcohol problem

If any of the above listed issues are of concern to you, you should set up a Retirement Protector Trust™ to protect your children or other beneficiaries. Set up your design appointment by calling my office at (760) 448-2220.

chapter nine

Real Life Case Examples

Imagine a couple. We will call them John and Sandy. John is 54 years old and Sandy is 55. John and Sandy have been married for 25 years and they have two young adult children, Max, who is 18 and Alexis, who is 21. John was the breadwinner in the family while Sandy took care of the kids at home and so all of the retirement accounts are in his name. John retired early since his company got purchased and he experienced the windfall of that transaction. John's IRA has about $700,000 in it. Although their children Max and Alexis are great kids with Alexis in college and Max getting ready to head off to college, they are still young and inexperienced and John and Sandy want to ensure that the kids don't make poor decisions with the money they will eventually inherit.

John and Sandy each set up a Retirement Protector Trust™. Each of their trusts is a revocable trust funded with $10 during their lifetimes. John has updated his beneficiary form for his IRA to list Sandy as the primary beneficiary and his Retirement Protector Trust™ as the contingent beneficiary with addendums to provide for a stretch-out for each of his children based on their individual life expectancies. In John and Sandy's Retirement Protector Trusts™, they have nominated a Successor Trustee (they are each their own current Trustee respectively while they are alive) to administer their trusts until each of their children has reached the age of 35. When a child reaches the age of 35, their separate share trust becomes "beneficiary-controlled".

Each child at that age can act as their own Trustee and continue to take only the annual RMD out based on a divisor in the Single Life Table published by the IRS for inherited IRAs, or they may take out more and accelerate distributions from their separate share of the IRA. John and Sandy want to give their children flexibility and control, but not until they are much more mature and more likely to make wise choices. Below is a table of the projected lifetime distributions to John as well as to his children (in this example, we used the life expectancy of his oldest child, Alexis, for convenience purposes for the inherited IRA stretch). Note that the original $700,000 account balance becomes over **$6,500,000** over their children's lifetimes. This clearly demonstrates the sheer power of the stretch-out in a tax deferred environment.

RMD Stretch IRAs by Year [-]

Total Distributions

Total projected distributions during owner's lifetime:	$1,600,226.49
Total projected distributions during beneficiary's lifetime:	$6,582,251.32
Total projected distributions:	$8,182,477.81

Owner and account information

Owner's birth date	10/11/1960 Age 54 as of 12/31/2014
Owner's life expectancy	42.6 years, calculated using the IRS uniform life expectancy table
Owner's age at death	85 as of 12/31/2045
Plan type	Traditional IRA
Previous year ending value	$700,000.00 as of 12/31/2013
Annual rate of return	6%

Beneficiary's Information

Beneficiary birth date	7/2/1993 Age 21 as of 12/31/2014
Is beneficiary a spouse?	no
Beneficiary's age at death	N/A
Spouse's beneficiary's birth date	N/A

Account Balances and Minimum Distributions by Year*

As of 12/31	Recipient	Year End Age	Previous Year End Cash Value	Life Expectancy	Required Minimum Distribution
2014	Owner	54	$700,000.00		$0.00
2015	Owner	55	$742,000.00		$0.00
2016	Owner	56	$786,520.00		$0.00
2017	Owner	57	$833,711.20		$0.00
2018	Owner	58	$883,733.87		$0.00
2019	Owner	59	$936,757.90		$0.00
2020	Owner	60	$992,963.37		$0.00
2021	Owner	61	$1,052,541.17		$0.00
2022	Owner	62	$1,115,693.64		$0.00
2023	Owner	63	$1,182,635.26		$0.00
2024	Owner	64	$1,253,593.38		$0.00
2025	Owner	65	$1,328,808.98		$0.00
2026	Owner	66	$1,408,537.52		$0.00
2027	Owner	67	$1,493,049.77		$0.00
2028	Owner	68	$1,582,632.76		$0.00
2029	Owner	69	$1,677,590.73		$0.00
2030	Owner	70	$1,778,246.17		$0.00
2031	Owner	71	$1,884,940.94	26.5	$71,129.85

Year	Role	Age	Value	Rate	Amount
2032	Owner	72	$1,926,907.55	25.6	$75,269.83
2033	Owner	73	$1,967,252.17	24.7	$79,645.84
2034	Owner	74	$2,005,641.46	23.8	$84,270.65
2035	Owner	75	$2,041,709.30	22.9	$89,157.61
2036	Owner	76	$2,075,054.25	22	$94,320.65
2037	Owner	77	$2,105,236.86	21.2	$99,303.63
2038	Owner	78	$2,132,247.44	20.3	$105,036.82
2039	Owner	79	$2,155,145.47	19.5	$110,520.28
2040	Owner	80	$2,173,933.92	18.7	$116,253.15
2041	Owner	81	$2,188,116.81	17.9	$122,241.16
2042	Owner	82	$2,197,162.66	17.1	$128,489.04
2043	Owner	83	$2,200,503.38	16.3	$135,000.21
2044	Owner	84	$2,197,533.37	15.5	$141,776.35
2045	Owner	85	$2,187,609.02	14.8	$147,811.42
2046	Beneficiary	53	$2,171,054.14	31.4	$69,141.85
2047	Beneficiary	54	$2,232,175.54	30.4	$73,426.83
2048	Beneficiary	55	$2,292,679.24	29.4	$77,982.29
2049	Beneficiary	56	$2,352,257.70	28.4	$82,825.98
2050	Beneficiary	57	$2,410,567.18	27.4	$87,976.90
2051	Beneficiary	58	$2,467,224.31	26.4	$93,455.47
2052	Beneficiary	59	$2,521,802.30	25.4	$99,283.56
2053	Beneficiary	60	$2,573,826.88	24.4	$105,484.71
2054	Beneficiary	61	$2,622,771.78	23.4	$112,084.26
2055	Beneficiary	62	$2,668,053.83	22.4	$119,109.55
2056	Beneficiary	63	$2,709,027.51	21.4	$126,590.07
2057	Beneficiary	64	$2,744,979.09	20.4	$134,557.80
2058	Beneficiary	65	$2,775,120.04	19.4	$143,047.42
2059	Beneficiary	66	$2,798,579.82	18.4	$152,096.73
2060	Beneficiary	67	$2,814,397.88	17.4	$161,747.00
2061	Beneficiary	68	$2,821,514.75	16.4	$172,043.58
2062	Beneficiary	69	$2,818,762.06	15.4	$183,036.50
2063	Beneficiary	70	$2,804,851.28	14.4	$194,781.34
2064	Beneficiary	71	$2,778,361.02	13.4	$207,340.37
2065	Beneficiary	72	$2,737,722.31	12.4	$220,784.06
2066	Beneficiary	73	$2,681,201.59	11.4	$235,193.12
2067	Beneficiary	74	$2,606,880.57	10.4	$250,661.59
2068	Beneficiary	75	$2,512,631.81	9.4	$267,301.26
2069	Beneficiary	76	$2,396,088.46	8.4	$285,248.63
2070	Beneficiary	77	$2,254,605.14	7.4	$304,676.37
2071	Beneficiary	78	$2,085,205.08	6.4	$325,813.29
2072	Beneficiary	79	$1,884,504.09	5.4	$348,982.24
2073	Beneficiary	80	$1,648,592.10	4.4	$374,680.02
2074	Beneficiary	81	$1,372,827.61	3.4	$403,772.83
2075	Beneficiary	82	$1,051,424.44	2.4	$438,093.52
2076	Beneficiary	83	$676,416.39	1.4	$483,154.56
2077	Beneficiary	84	$233,846.81	0.4	$247,877.62

*All distributions are assumed to be taken at the end of the year. If you have questions, please consult with your own tax advisor regarding your specific situation. Information provided by http://www.dinkytown.net/java/StretchIRA.html.

In our second case example, imagine Fred. Fred is now 72 years old. Fred is unmarried and he doesn't have children, but he does have a niece and a nephew for which he is fond of. He knows that he is unlikely to use up the entire balance of his $1,100,000 IRA because of the size of the account and because he has other assets. He also doesn't need more than the annual RMD from his IRA to live comfortably. Fred's niece Cindy is 47 and his nephew Bob is 48. Fred decides to set up a Retirement Protector Trust™ to protect his niece and nephew, especially since Cindy has gone through a divorce and he doesn't want a new spouse to have access to the money in the IRA that he wants to leave to her and to Bob. Fred has asked his attorney to act as Trust Protector so that she can easily respond to changing circumstances within the trust for creditor protection such as switching on the power to accumulate RMDs inside the trust and to fill a vacancy if there is no Trustee able or willing to act. Below is a summary of the power of the tax deferral for Fred's $1,100,000 IRA.

Minimum Required Distribution for 2014 is $42,968.75 RMD

The account owner will be over 70 1/2 by the end of this year, resulting in a $42,968.75 RMD for 2014.

RMD Stretch IRAs by Year	[-]
Total Distributions	
Total projected distributions during owner's lifetime:	$487,390.43
Total projected distributions during beneficiary's lifetime:	$3,313,458.96
Total projected distributions:	$3,800,849.39
Owner and account information	
Owner's birth date	12/2/1942 Age 72 as of 12/31/2014
Owner's life expectancy	25.6 years, calculated using the IRS uniform life expectancy table
Owner's age at death	80 as of 12/31/2022
Plan type	Traditional IRA
Previous year ending value	$1,100,000.00 as of 12/31/2013
Annual rate of return	6%
Beneficiary's Information	
Beneficiary birth date	7/5/1966 Age 48 as of 12/31/2014
Is beneficiary a spouse?	no
Beneficiary's age at death	N/A
Spouse's beneficiary's birth date	N/A

Account Balances and Minimum Distributions by Year*

As of 12/31	Recipient	Year End Age	Previous Year End Cash Value	Life Expectancy	Required Minimum Distribution
2014	Owner	72	$1,100,000.00	25.6	$42,968.75
2015	Owner	73	$1,123,031.25	24.7	$45,466.85
2016	Owner	74	$1,144,946.28	23.8	$48,106.99
2017	Owner	75	$1,165,536.07	22.9	$50,896.77
2018	Owner	76	$1,184,571.46	22	$53,844.16
2019	Owner	77	$1,201,801.59	21.2	$56,688.75
2020	Owner	78	$1,217,220.94	20.3	$59,961.62
2021	Owner	79	$1,230,292.58	19.5	$63,091.93
2022	Owner	80	$1,241,018.20	18.7	$66,364.61
2023	Beneficiary	57	$1,249,114.68	27.9	$44,771.14
2024	Beneficiary	58	$1,279,290.42	26.9	$47,557.26
2025	Beneficiary	59	$1,308,490.59	25.9	$50,520.87
2026	Beneficiary	60	$1,336,479.16	24.9	$53,673.86
2027	Beneficiary	61	$1,362,994.05	23.9	$57,029.04
2028	Beneficiary	62	$1,387,744.65	22.9	$60,600.20
2029	Beneficiary	63	$1,410,409.13	21.9	$64,402.24
2030	Beneficiary	64	$1,430,631.44	20.9	$68,451.27
2031	Beneficiary	65	$1,448,018.06	19.9	$72,764.73
2032	Beneficiary	66	$1,462,134.41	18.9	$77,361.61
2033	Beneficiary	67	$1,472,500.86	17.9	$82,262.62
2034	Beneficiary	68	$1,478,588.29	16.9	$87,490.43
2035	Beneficiary	69	$1,479,813.16	15.9	$93,070.01

Year		Age	Balance	Divisor	Distribution
2036	Beneficiary	70	$1,475,531.94	14.9	$99,028.99
2037	Beneficiary	71	$1,465,034.87	13.9	$105,398.19
2038	Beneficiary	72	$1,447,538.77	12.9	$112,212.31
2039	Beneficiary	73	$1,422,178.79	11.9	$119,510.82
2040	Beneficiary	74	$1,387,998.70	10.9	$127,339.33
2041	Beneficiary	75	$1,343,939.29	9.9	$135,751.44
2042	Beneficiary	76	$1,288,824.21	8.9	$144,811.71
2043	Beneficiary	77	$1,221,341.95	7.9	$154,600.25
2044	Beneficiary	78	$1,140,022.22	6.9	$165,220.61
2045	Beneficiary	79	$1,043,202.94	5.9	$176,814.06
2046	Beneficiary	80	$928,981.06	4.9	$189,587.97
2047	Beneficiary	81	$795,131.95	3.9	$203,879.99
2048	Beneficiary	82	$638,959.88	2.9	$220,330.99
2049	Beneficiary	83	$456,966.48	1.9	$240,508.67
2050	Beneficiary	84	$243,875.80	0.9	$258,508.35

As you can see, Fred's niece and nephew's projected distributions would be about $3,300,000 if stretched through the trust.

*All distributions are assumed to be taken at the end of the year. If you have questions, please consult with your own tax advisor regarding your specific situation. Information provided by http://www.dinkytown.net/java/StretchIRA.html.

In our last case example, let's examine a married couple with minor children. The couple's names are Mike and Susan. Mike and Susan both work and are age 45 and 44 respectively. Mike is a scientist at a local biotech company and has a 401(K) with a balance of $156,000 and an IRA rollover from a prior employer with a balance of about $75,000. Susan is a nurse at the local hospital and has a 403B account with about $80,000 and a 401(K) with a balance of $25,000. In total, the two combined have amassed $336,000 in their retirement accounts. Mike and Susan have one child named Tommy. Tommy is 10 years old. Mike and Susan have already set up their revocable trust with some asset protection planning for Tommy that will protect the money, house and life insurance that they will be leaving to him, but they are also concerned about the money in the retirement accounts, in particular that Tommy could blow the stretch-out when he reaches the age of 18 and that the money in those accounts could be taken in a divorce if Tommy ever got married. Below illustrates the power of deferral that they are giving to their son by protecting their retirement accounts for him through a Retirement Protector Trust™. The results are pretty stunning. For this case, assume that Susan is the surviving spouse, she rolls over Mike's accounts at his death and she lives to the age of 85. Note, this couple is still relatively young and will likely contribute even more to their retirement accounts in the next 15-20 years. But for this example, let's assume they never add any additional money to their retirement accounts. The $336,000 turns into **$5,857,672** at an average annual rate of 6% in total projected distributions during Tommy's life. Essentially, they are providing him a <u>paycheck for life</u>. And if Tommy doesn't consume all of the accounts during his lifetime, Tommy's children can benefit under the same terms of the trust.

Minimum Required Distribution for 2014 is $0.00 RMD

The account owner will not be over 70 1/2 by the end of this year, resulting in a $0.00 RMD for 2014

RMD Stretch IRAs by Year [-]

Total Distributions	
Total projected distributions during owner's lifetime:	$1,375,565.79
Total projected distributions during beneficiary's lifetime:	$5,857,672.53
Total projected distributions:	$7,233,238.32

Owner and account information	
Owner's birth date	7/1/1970 Age 44 as of 12/31/2014
Owner's life expectancy	52.4 years, calculated using the IRS uniform life expectancy table
Owner's age at death	85 as of 12/31/2055
Plan type	Traditional IRA
Previous year ending value	$336,000.00 as of 12/31/2013
Annual rate of return	6%

Beneficiary's Information	
Beneficiary birth date	6/2/2004 Age 10 as of 12/31/2014
Is beneficiary a spouse?	no
Beneficiary's age at death	N/A
Spouse's beneficiary's birth date	N/A

Account Balances and Minimum Distributions by Year*

As of 12/31	Recipient	Year End Age	Previous Year End Cash Value	Life Expectancy	Required Minimum Distribution
2014	Owner	44	$336,000.00		$0.00
2015	Owner	45	$356,160.00		$0.00
2016	Owner	46	$377,529.60		$0.00
2017	Owner	47	$400,181.38		$0.00
2018	Owner	48	$424,192.26		$0.00
2019	Owner	49	$449,643.80		$0.00
2020	Owner	50	$476,622.43		$0.00
2021	Owner	51	$505,219.78		$0.00
2022	Owner	52	$535,532.97		$0.00
2023	Owner	53	$567,664.95		$0.00
2024	Owner	54	$601,724.85		$0.00
2025	Owner	55	$637,828.34		$0.00
2026	Owner	56	$676,098.04		$0.00
2027	Owner	57	$716,663.92		$0.00
2028	Owner	58	$759,663.76		$0.00
2029	Owner	59	$805,243.59		$0.00
2030	Owner	60	$853,558.21		$0.00
2031	Owner	61	$904,771.70		$0.00
2032	Owner	62	$959,058.00		$0.00
2033	Owner	63	$1,016,601.48		$0.00
2034	Owner	64	$1,077,597.57		$0.00
2035	Owner	65	$1,142,253.42		$0.00
2036	Owner	66	$1,210,788.63		$0.00
2037	Owner	67	$1,283,435.95		$0.00
2038	Owner	68	$1,360,442.11		$0.00

2039	Owner	69	$1,442,068.64		$0.00
2040	Owner	70	$1,528,592.76		$0.00
2041	Owner	71	$1,620,308.33	26.5	$61,143.71
2042	Owner	72	$1,656,383.12	25.6	$64,702.47
2043	Owner	73	$1,691,063.64	24.7	$68,464.11
2044	Owner	74	$1,724,063.35	23.8	$72,439.64
2045	Owner	75	$1,755,067.51	22.9	$76,640.50
2046	Owner	76	$1,783,731.06	22	$81,078.68
2047	Owner	77	$1,809,676.24	21.2	$85,362.09
2048	Owner	78	$1,832,894.72	20.3	$90,290.38
2049	Owner	79	$1,852,578.02	19.5	$95,004.00
2050	Owner	80	$1,868,728.70	18.7	$99,932.02
2051	Owner	81	$1,880,920.40	17.9	$105,079.35
2052	Owner	82	$1,888,696.27	17.1	$110,450.07
2053	Owner	83	$1,891,567.98	16.3	$116,047.12
2054	Owner	84	$1,889,014.94	15.5	$121,871.93
2055	Owner	85	$1,880,483.91	14.8	$127,059.72
2056	Beneficiary	52	$1,866,253.22	32.3	$57,778.74
2057	Beneficiary	53	$1,920,449.67	31.3	$61,356.22
2058	Beneficiary	54	$1,974,320.43	30.3	$65,159.09
2059	Beneficiary	55	$2,027,620.57	29.3	$69,202.07
2060	Beneficiary	56	$2,080,075.73	28.3	$73,500.91
2061	Beneficiary	57	$2,131,379.36	27.3	$78,072.50
2062	Beneficiary	58	$2,181,189.62	26.3	$82,934.97
2063	Beneficiary	59	$2,229,126.03	25.3	$88,107.75
2064	Beneficiary	60	$2,274,765.84	24.3	$93,611.76
2065	Beneficiary	61	$2,317,640.03	23.3	$99,469.53
2066	Beneficiary	62	$2,357,228.90	22.3	$105,705.33
2067	Beneficiary	63	$2,392,957.30	21.3	$112,345.41
2068	Beneficiary	64	$2,424,189.33	20.3	$119,418.19
2069	Beneficiary	65	$2,450,222.50	19.3	$126,954.53
2070	Beneficiary	66	$2,470,281.32	18.3	$134,988.05
2071	Beneficiary	67	$2,483,510.15	17.3	$143,555.50
2072	Beneficiary	68	$2,488,965.26	16.3	$152,697.26
2073	Beneficiary	69	$2,485,605.92	15.3	$162,457.90
2074	Beneficiary	70	$2,472,284.38	14.3	$172,887.02
2075	Beneficiary	71	$2,447,734.42	13.3	$184,040.18
2076	Beneficiary	72	$2,410,558.31	12.3	$195,980.35
2077	Beneficiary	73	$2,359,211.46	11.3	$208,779.78
2078	Beneficiary	74	$2,291,984.37	10.3	$222,522.75
2079	Beneficiary	75	$2,206,980.68	9.3	$237,309.75
2080	Beneficiary	76	$2,102,089.77	8.3	$253,263.83
2081	Beneficiary	77	$1,974,951.33	7.3	$270,541.28
2082	Beneficiary	78	$1,822,907.13	6.3	$289,350.34
2083	Beneficiary	79	$1,642,931.22	5.3	$309,987.02
2084	Beneficiary	80	$1,431,520.07	4.3	$332,911.64
2085	Beneficiary	81	$1,184,499.63	3.3	$358,939.28
2086	Beneficiary	82	$896,630.33	2.3	$389,839.27
2087	Beneficiary	83	$560,588.88	1.3	$431,222.22
2088	Beneficiary	84	$163,001.99	0.3	$172,782.11

*All distributions are assumed to be taken at the end of the year. If you have questions, please consult with your own tax advisor regarding your specific situation. Information provided by http://www.dinkytown.net/java/StretchIRA.html.

chapter ten

What is the Process to Set up a Retirement Protector Trust™?

The process to set up your Retirement Protector Trust™ is simple. All we need from you is a short questionnaire completed along with a list of your retirement accounts, the custodians, and the balances in each. If you are married, we will set up two separate trusts. Typically, for married couples, each will want to list their spouse as the primary beneficiary and their new Retirement Protector Trust™ as the contingent beneficiary on each retirement account. Don't worry, we take care of that for you. The reason is that most of the time our clients have more than one child or beneficiary they would like to benefit from the trust, so we draft special language on an addendum that we attach to the change of beneficiary form after you have executed your trust document.

Then, once you have signed your change of beneficiary form, we will "certify mail" your beneficiary form along with a copy of the trust to your plan administrator. Within a few short weeks, you should receive a confirmation of the updated beneficiaries on your retirement accounts from each plan administrator. When you receive a confirmation, we ask that you please provide us a copy for our file and that you place the original in your Retirement Protector Trust™ binder for safekeeping. If you close an account and open another retirement account, we request that you let us know so that we may help you fill out your beneficiary designation form so that your Retirement Protector Trust™ is properly designated as a beneficiary.

The trust can be drafted as an irrevocable or a revocable trust. Typically, for convenience purposes, we draft them as revocable so that you may amend your trust document in the future as need be.

We also strongly recommend designating a Trust Protector (see chapter 6) in your trust document so that the power to accumulate the RMDs inside your trust can be turned on and/or a vacancy in the Trusteeship can be later filled.

You will also want to be thinking about whether or not you'd like your children to be their own Trustees at a certain point in time. For some, this is a good option. For others who, for instance, have a special needs beneficiary or a child who has poor financial decision-making skills, may wish to only have other trustees in charge for their child's lifetime. If the latter is desired, you will want to consider having a corporate trustee in place either as your first choice or as a back-up to ensure continuity of management as your child ages.

chapter eleven

Operating Guidelines for Your Retirement Protector Trust™

There are certain requirements during your lifetime and beyond that will need to be met in order for your Retirement Protector Trust™ to be successful. These guidelines are only a summary and not a detailed outline of every necessary thing that will be required of you or your Successor Trustee. Therefore it is very important that your Successor Trustee obtain *competent* legal counsel regarding the administration of your Retirement Protector Trust™ down the road.

Once you sign your Retirement Protector Trust™, it will only be initially funded with an arbitrary amount (to ensure it is valid under the law). Typically we fund it with $10. You will not be transferring your retirement accounts into the name of the Retirement Protector Trust™. But your beneficiary forms will need to be updated. If you are married, you will likely want to list your spouse as the primary beneficiary on your retirement accounts and list your Retirement Protector Trust™ as the contingent beneficiary. In our office, we do this updating for you. There are typically addendums that we prepare to be filed with the updated beneficiary form to ensure maximum income-tax deferral of your retirement accounts based on each beneficiary's individual life expectancy.

Once we have updated the beneficiary form and attached the addendum, we send the beneficiary change form documents and a copy of your Retirement Protector Trust™ to your retirement plan custodian by Certified Mail with return receipt requested to ensure their receipt of the change. Normally, the plan custodian will send you a confirmation letter evidencing the change once they have updated their system. However, we maintain a signed copy of the beneficiary change form in our records as well. If you are married, we will need to create a trust for both you and your spouse. Note too that if you change plan custodians, transfer your retirement account to a different account, or create a new retirement account, the beneficiary designation form will need to be completed in the same fashion again. If you are married and one spouse dies and the surviving spouse rolls over the account, he or she will need to update the beneficiary designation form to list *their* Retirement Protector Trust™ as the primary beneficiary of the account. If you are single, you will likely want to list your Retirement Protector Trust™ as the primary beneficiary.

If your Retirement Protector Trust™ is drafted as a revocable trust, you may update the provisions of the trust at any time by amendment, signed and notarized. In such a case, you will want to make sure to review your Retirement Protector Trust™ with your attorney along with your estate plan every 2-3 years. Things like a change in your family situation, an increase in your net-worth, or a change in the tax law could significantly impact the effectiveness of your estate plan, so make sure to stay in touch with your attorney. If the trust is drafted as an irrevocable trust, you will not be able to amend your trust, but remember that you may always update the beneficiary designation form on your retirement account.

After you have passed away, your Retirement Protector Trust™ must be administered in a timely fashion to ensure optimization of the tax and asset protection benefits associated with your Retirement Protector Trust™. Your Successor Trustee should first consult with *competent* legal counsel, as well as tax and financial advisory counsel. It will be important for your attorney to review not only the Retirement Protector Trust™, but your entire estate plan to ensure maximum estate tax benefits.

One important note—I recommend that NO WITHDRAWALS be made from your retirement account after your passing until your Successor Trustee has had an opportunity to meet with your attorney to discuss their recommendations. Extremely important tax elections can be lost once withdrawals are made and could harm the plan that you so carefully took the time to set up. We also recommend that the Successor Trustee does not contact the beneficiaries of the Retirement Protector Trust™ or the plan custodians of the retirement accounts prior to this important review meeting with your attorney.

Depending on how large your estate is at your death, there may be a need to file a 706 Death Tax Return, which is typically due within nine months of date of death. The Successor Trustee of your Retirement Protector Trust™ will want to coordinate with the Trustee of your living trust to ensure all appropriate tax returns and exemption allocations are done. Your Successor Trustee will also want to engage a competent CPA to handle the final income tax return and trust return filings.

There are a few important dates to remember regarding your Retirement Protector Trust™ as well. The first of which is that if you were required to take Required Minimum Distributions out while you were alive (i.e., because you are over 70 ½), your Successor Trustee of your Retirement Protector Trust™ will need to check with your retirement plan custodian to ensure that the withdrawal for the year in death has been distributed from the account. If the distribution is not made in that calendar year, there will likely be a large penalty.

Also, note that a non-spousal beneficiary will need to commence RMD withdrawals by **December 31st** in the year following your death in order to utilize the stretch-out of the account. Also, as mentioned in the prior chapter on Trust Protectors, the Trust Protector must make his or her affirmative election to turn on the power to accumulate if so desired within 9 months of your date of death (if a conduit trust with optional accumulation powers is drafted). Your Successor Trustee should consult with your attorney regarding this matter before anything is done.

chapter twelve

About the Author

BRENDA GEIGER, J.D.
Managing Attorney, Geiger Law Office, P.C.

Mrs. Geiger's practice is located in Carlsbad, California. Her firm focuses on mid-level and high-end Estate Planning, Asset Protection, Business Planning, Trust Administration, and Elder Law. She obtained her law degree from the University of San Diego School of Law where she served as an Editor and author on the board of the San Diego International Law Journal.

Mrs. Geiger is involved in a variety of professional and community organizations. She serves as an editor for the North County San Diego Bar Association Magazine (The North County Lawyer). She is an active member of the North County Estate Planning Council, North County Bar Association, STAR San Diego, WealthCounsel, LLC, and ElderCounsel, LLC. She is also a nationally recognized speaker.

Additionally, Mrs. Geiger is the author of four other books. Her first book on estate planning was *Safeguarding the Nest*, (now in its Third Edition) and her book on Elder Law planning is titled *How to Avoid the Catastrophic Costs and Effects of Long Term Care: a California Elder Law Guide*. In 2013, she published a book to help closely held business owners titled *"Protecting You and Your Business, a Practical Guide for California Business Owners."* Her most recent book *Secrets of Great Estate Planning* was published in June of 2014. She is also the author of the Law Review article "Authorization to Kill Terrorist Leaders and Those Who Harbor Them: An International Analysis of Defensive Assassination," *San Diego International Law Journal, 4 San Diego Int'l L.J. 491*, Spring 2003, and several other articles.

Mrs. Geiger is admitted to practice before the United States Federal Court for the Ninth District and California State Courts and is an accredited V.A. Planning Attorney. On a more personal note, Brenda is married to Len, the CEO of a San Diego based technology company, and has two young children. She loves running, travel and spending time with her family.

She can be reached for news interview inquires, speaking event requests and private client meetings at (760) 448-2220 or through her firm's contact page at www.geigerlawoffice.net.

Geiger Law Office, P.C.
1917 Palomar Oaks Way, Suite 160
Carlsbad, CA 92008

(760) 448-2220
www.geigerlawoffice.net
info@geigerlawoffice.net

Geiger Law Office, P.C.
1917 Palomar Oaks Way, Suite 160
Carlsbad, CA 92008

(760) 448-2220
www.geigerlawoffice.net
info@geigerlawoffice.net

WA